LOOKING THROUGH LAY[...]

Change one letter in [...]
seek to find.

S	E	E	K
F	I	N	D

Plant this to get a flower.

Do this to a letter or text message.

Do this to something torn or broken.

Use this to memorize Jeremiah 29:13.

Now, find one more thing! Look for
Jeremiah 29:13 in your own Bible.
Write it here:

Jesus Was Born

Hundreds of years before Jesus was born, God told prophets to write about His plan to send His Son to be our Savior. Many years later an angel of the Lord appeared to Joseph. The angel told him Mary would have God's Son, and they were to name Him Jesus. Just as God promised Jesus was born in Bethlehem. God promised He would send His Son, and He did.

Isaiah 7:14; Micah 5:2;
Matthew 1:18—2:6

Jesus is the Savior God promised.

Bethlehem means house of bread. It's about five miles southwest of Jerusalem.

PROMISE MADE, PROMISE KEPT

What promises did God make about the coming of Jesus? How did He keep those promises?

Promise Made

_____
_____
_____
_____

Promise Kept

_____
_____
_____
_____

JUST THE ARTI-FACTS

Jars like this were discovered in 11 different caves near Qumran, a site on the northwestern shore of the Dead Sea. The sealed jars contained scrolls with the same words you can find in your Bible!

Qumran

Jesus Healed a Blind Man

Prophets wrote about what would happen when God's Son came to earth. They wrote about miracles He would perform such as healing people. When Jesus began His ministry, He did everything God said He would do. One day while in Jerusalem, Jesus passed a man who had been blind since birth. Jesus spat on the ground and made some mud. He spread the mud over the man's eyes and told the man to go wash in the Pool of Siloam. The man did as he was told, and he could see! The man told people what Jesus had done. Later, when the man saw Jesus, he worshiped Him.

Psalm 146:8; Isaiah 35:5-6a; John 9:1-41

Jesus has the power God promised

In today's story, Jesus told the blind man to go wash in the Pool of Siloam.
In 2004, the site of the original pool was found and it can be visited today!

4

TRENCHES TO TREASURE

Pick any trowel. Follow its trench to a treasure—a story about Jesus' power. (Find the whole story in your Bible!)

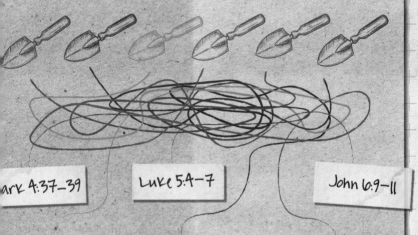

ark 4:37–39

Luke 5:4–7

John 6:9–11

Mark 7:32–35

Luke 17:12–14

Matthew 14:23–25

JUST THE ARTI-FACTS

Here's how the Pool of Siloam looks now. It may have been used as a source of fresh water for part of Jerusalem.

Jesus Experienced Betrayal and Rejection

Jesus shared one last special supper with His disciples. During the meal Jesus explained that one of the disciples would betray Him. Jesus knew His betrayal and death would fulfill God's plan. After the meal, Jesus and all the disciples except for Judas went to the garden in Gethsemane. While they were there, Judas brought the soldiers to arrest Jesus and take Him to the high priest to begin the trials the prophets had written about many years before. Pilate, the Roman governor, tried to find a way to release Jesus, but the crowd shouted, "Crucify Him!" Jesus remained silent just as the prophecy said He would. Finally, Pilate gave in to the people's demands, and Jesus was handed over to the soldiers to be crucified.

Psalm 41:9; Isaiah 53:3,7; John 13; 18:1—19:16

Jesus knew what would happen and still followed God's plan.

If Jesus' disciples wore shoes like this, no wonder their feet needed washing! In those days, a good host would provide water, or tell a servant to wash a guest's feet. Jesus volunteered to do that job without being asked.

6

SITE TO SITE

Jesus visited these sites before He was taken to be crucified. Draw a line that connects them in the right order.

Gethsemane

Pilate's house
(Roman governor)

Golgotha
(place of crucifixion)

Upper room
(last supper with disciples)

Caiaphas' house

JUST THE ARTI-FACTS

Next to these steps leading to Caiaphas' house are caves where Jesus would likely have been held as a prisoner.

MATERIAL MATCH

When you match the material fragments, you'll have an Old Testament prophecy about Jesus and a New Testament verse that shows how He fulfilled it. Check each match off the list as you find it.

Isaiah 9:1–2

Jeremiah 23:6

Psalm 110:1

Mark 16:19

John 10:14

Mark 15:24

Psalm 22:18

Zechariah 9:9

Matthew 1:20–21

Isaiah 40:11

Matthew 4:12–16

Matthew 21:7

- ☐ Jesus saves people from their sins.
- ☐ Jesus lived in Galilee.
- ☐ Jesus said that He is the Good Shepherd.
- ☐ Jesus entered Jerusalem on a donkey.
- ☐ Soldiers gambled for Jesus' clothing.
- ☐ Jesus was greatly honored by God.

Jesus Is Alive

God told prophets that Jesus would be born and that He would die for our sins. God also said that Jesus would die with the wicked, be buried with the rich, and be raised from the dead. Just as God said, Jesus was crucified between two criminals and Joseph of Arimathea, a wealthy man, buried Jesus' body in Joseph's tomb. A stone was rolled in front of the tomb. On the first day of the week, Mary Magdalene went to the tomb. The stone had been rolled away, and Jesus was gone. Peter and John came to the tomb and saw the burial clothes, but Jesus was not there. While Mary stood outside the tomb crying, a man she thought was a gardener appeared. The Man called her name and immediately Mary knew He was Jesus. She couldn't wait to tell the disciples that Jesus is alive!

Isaiah 53:5,9-11; John 19:17—20:18

Jesus fulfilled God's plan to be our Savior.

This is myrrh. It was used to make oils and perfumes and to make stinky clothes smell better. Nicodemus brought 75 pounds of myrrh and aloe powder to prepare Jesus' body for burial.

10

PEOPLE PLACEMENT

Do you remember how these people played a part in the story of Jesus' burial and resurrection?

Nicodemus and Joseph of Arimathea

Mary Magdalene

Jesus

John & Peter

JUST THE ARTI-FACTS

Wealthy Jewish families would purchase a cave like this for burial of family members. Some even had rooms branching off a main hallway. A special track was cut in the ground so that a large stone could be rolled to open or close the entrance.

Philip Told The Good News

While Philip was preaching in Samaria, an angel of the Lord told him to go south to the road that goes to Gaza. Philip obeyed the angel. Philip saw a man traveling in a chariot. The man was reading a copy of the Isaiah scroll. Philip asked the man if he understood what he was reading. The man said he did not and that he needed someone to explain it to him. Philip explained the good news about Jesus to the man. The man believed what Philip told him and believed in Jesus. Philip baptized the man, and the man went on his way rejoicing.

Isaiah 53:7-8; Acts 8:26-40

The Bible is true and helps us tell others about Jesus.

How would you like to write a story, then watch the words fall off the page? Flaky ink was a problem in Bible times if you were writing on parchment. But someone discovered a mixture of nutgalls from an oak tree and iron sulfate would make their words stick!

Nutgalls

RETURN AND REPORT

After VBS, you can report your discoveries about Jesus! Toss a coin—heads for 1 space, tails for 2. Who can you tell? What will you tell?

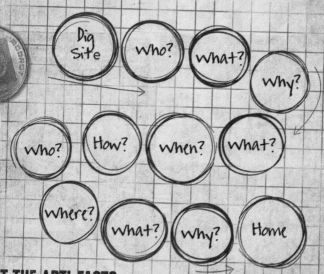

- Dig Site
- Who?
- What?
- Why?
- Who?
- How?
- When?
- What?
- Where?
- What?
- Why?
- Home

JUST THE ARTI-FACTS

This is the best preserved and largest scroll found in Qumran in 1947 (734 centimeters—that's 24 feet). It contains the entire book of Isaiah—the book you can find in your own Bible!

BRUSH OFF YOUR BIBLE!

Don't let dust settle on your Bible after VBS! Write your initials and the date on the tag after you read each story! Brush off these stories and you'll find ...

A TALKING DONKEY

Numbers 22:22–34

A NINE-FOOT GIANT

1 Samuel 17:3–49

THE SUN STOOD STILL

Joshua 10:6–14

A MYSTERIOUS HAND

Daniel 5:5–12

A SHIPWRECK

Acts
27:13-25

A CENTURION'S STORY

Matthew
8:5-13

COURAGEOUS BUILDERS

Nehemiah
4:4-14

A FISHY MIRACLE

John
21:3-11

NATION DIG

CLOSE EXAMINATION

Here are extreme close-ups of some artifacts you've examined all this week. Can you identify them without looking back? Do you remember the Bible story related to the artifact?

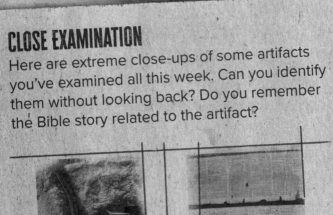